Destination CUBA

Traveling Coloring Book:

Relax, Color and Take a Virtual Vacation

SensationalCuba.com

TravelingColoringBook.com Series™
http://TravelingColoringBooks.com

BRUCE OLIVER

Travel Advisor & TV Host

Scent-Sational Travel & Food Resource Books™
Sensational Travel & Food Adult Coloring Books™

Axis Mundi Systems LLC dba Cruise with Bruce Enterprises

This Book Belongs to:

_____

- There are 30 pages for you to color as you take your Virtual Vacation.

- Each page has a description of where the photograph was taken to make the illustration.

- The illustration does not fill the page just in case you want to frame your masterpiece.

- You can order your next Destination Coloring Book by going to:

    http://TravelingColoringBooks.com

Bruce Oliver
Traveling Coloring Books

Copyright © 2017 by Bruce Oliver, TravelingColoringBook.com ™
Published by Vegas New Media Publishing Co., Las Vegas, NV

All rights reserved. No part of this book may be reproduced in any form without permission in writing written for inclusion in a magazine, newspaper, or any other informational media. Proper credits required.

First edition 2017

The illustrations used throughout the book are the property of the author. Each illustration has been rendered from photographs taken by the author and turned into the line art used to color.

For more information about Bruce Oliver please visit the following websites:

http://ScratchAndSniffTravel.com
http://BruceOliverTV.com
http://ScentSationalCuba.com
http://SensationalCuba.com

Printed in the United States of America.
ISBN-13: 978-1970029024 (Vegas New Wave Media)
ISBN-10: 1970029021

Book your next trip or cruise by going to:
http://BruceOliverTV.com
and click on the CRUISE or VACATION menu choice at the top of the page

Bruce Oliver with the Sones y Boleros de Cuba Band - Bar near Plaza Vieja - Havana, Cuba

Drinking some Havana Club at a Bar near Plaza Vieja - Havana, Cuba

Terminal Sierra Maestra in Plaza San Francisco - Havana, Cuba

Vintage cars along the Malecón / Sea wall in Havana, Cuba

Old Church now repurposed near Marti Park in Cienfuegos, Cuba

Pineapple, shrimp, rice and green beans

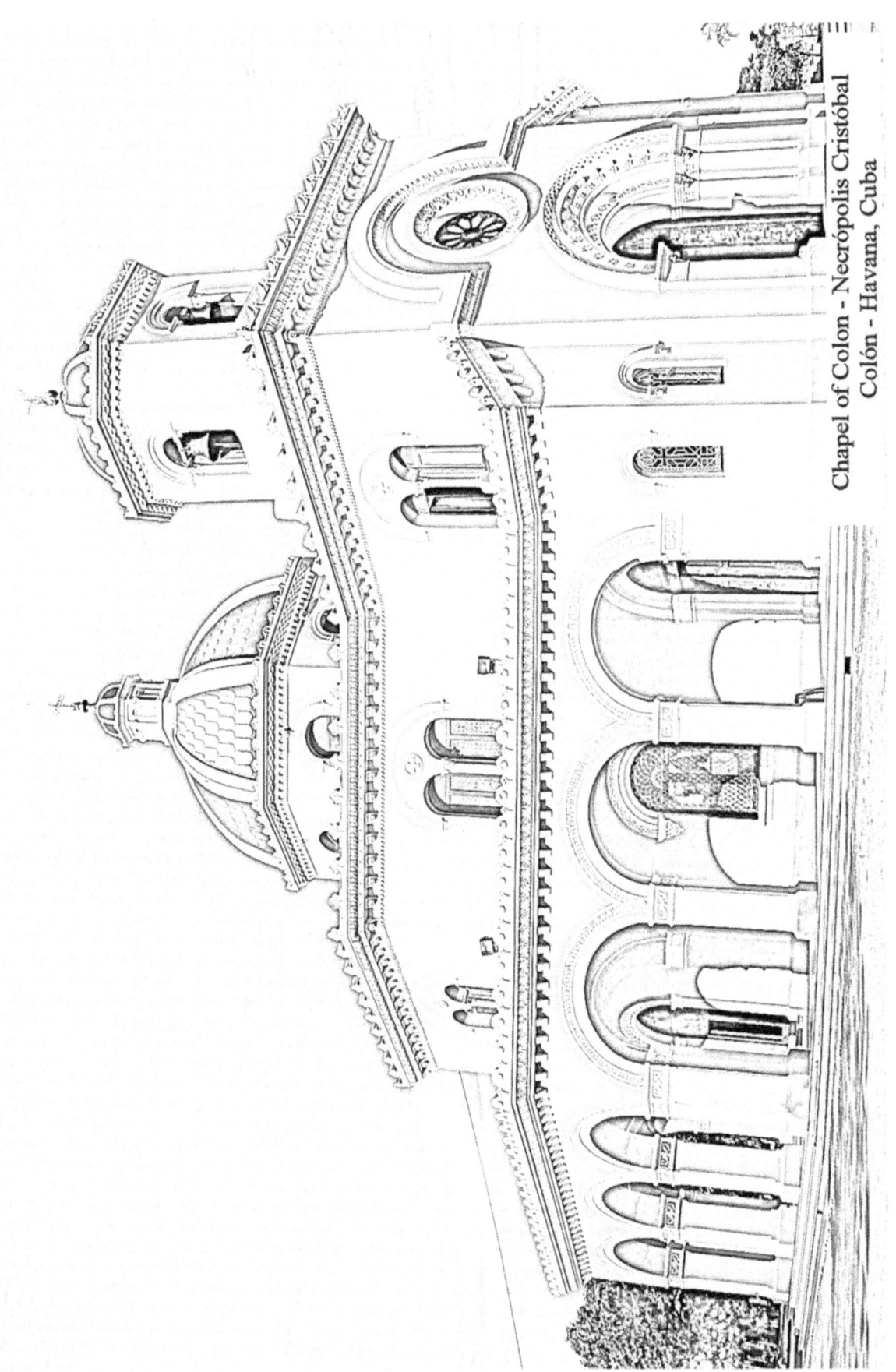

Chapel of Colon - Necrópolis Cristóbal Colón - Havana, Cuba

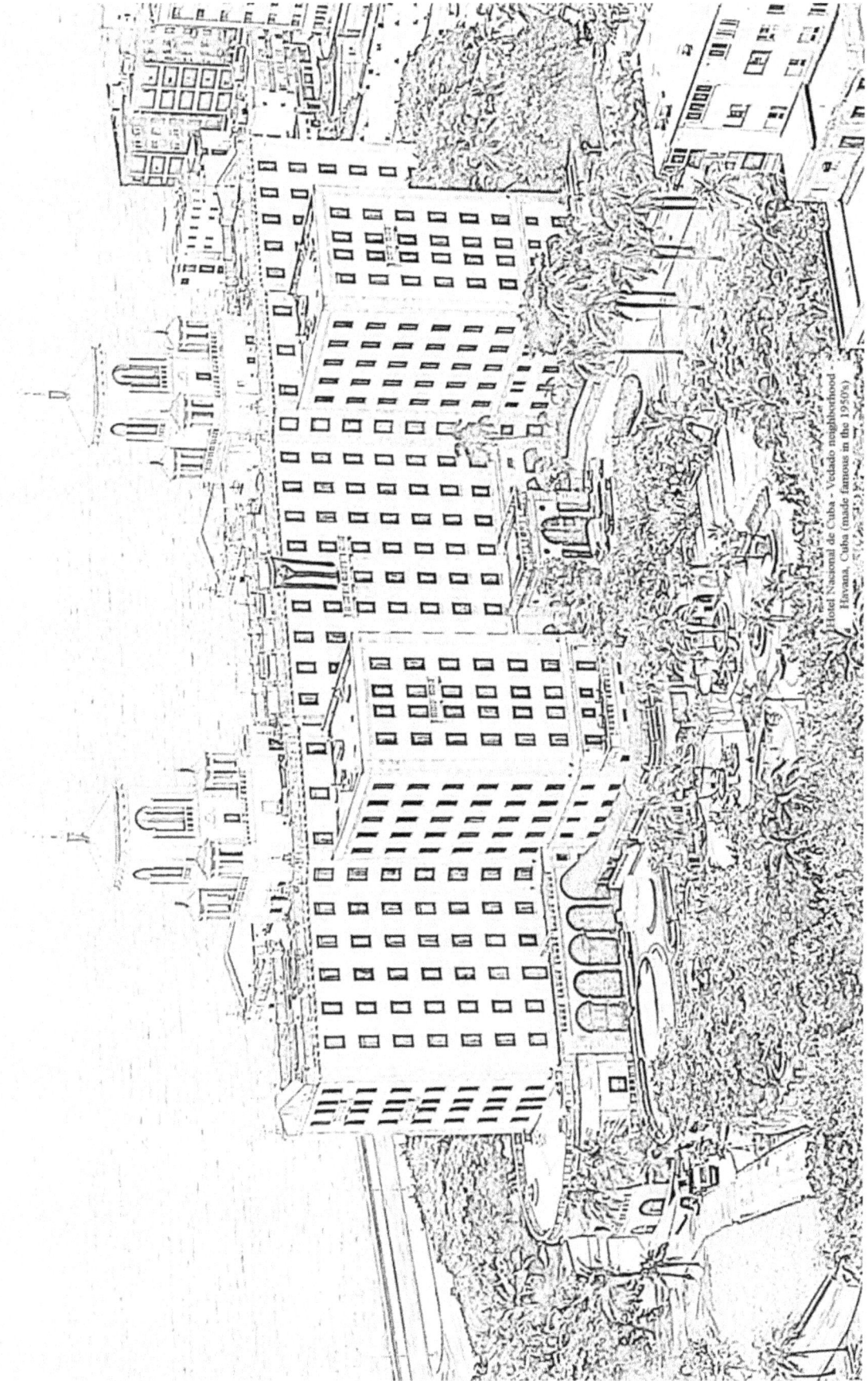

Hotel Nacional de Cuba - Vedado neighborhood
Havana, Cuba (made famous in the 1950s)

Entertainers in Plaza San Francisco - Havana, Cuba

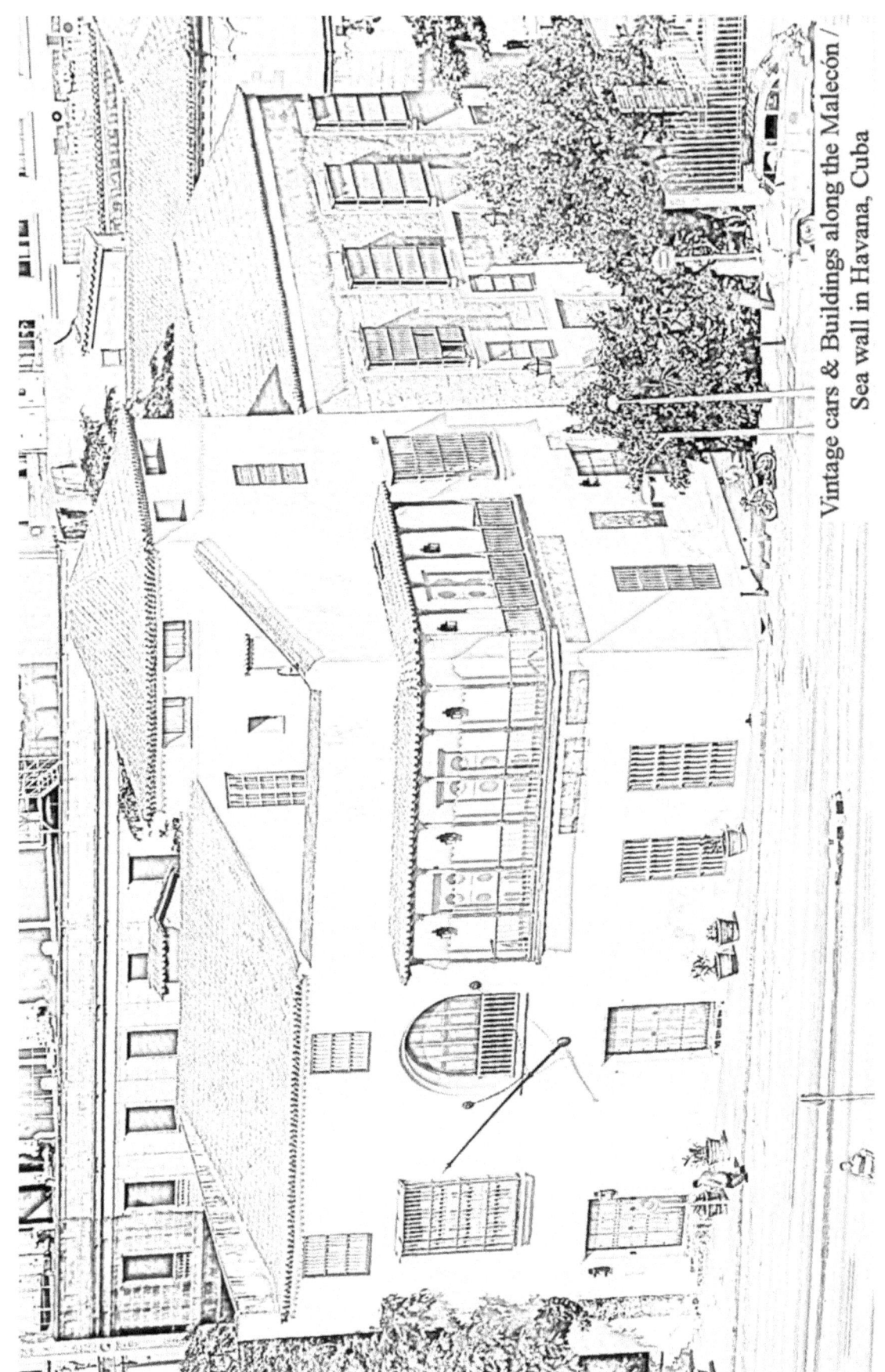

Vintage cars & Buildings along the Malecón / Sea wall in Havana, Cuba

City Hall near Marti Park in Cienfuegos, Cuba

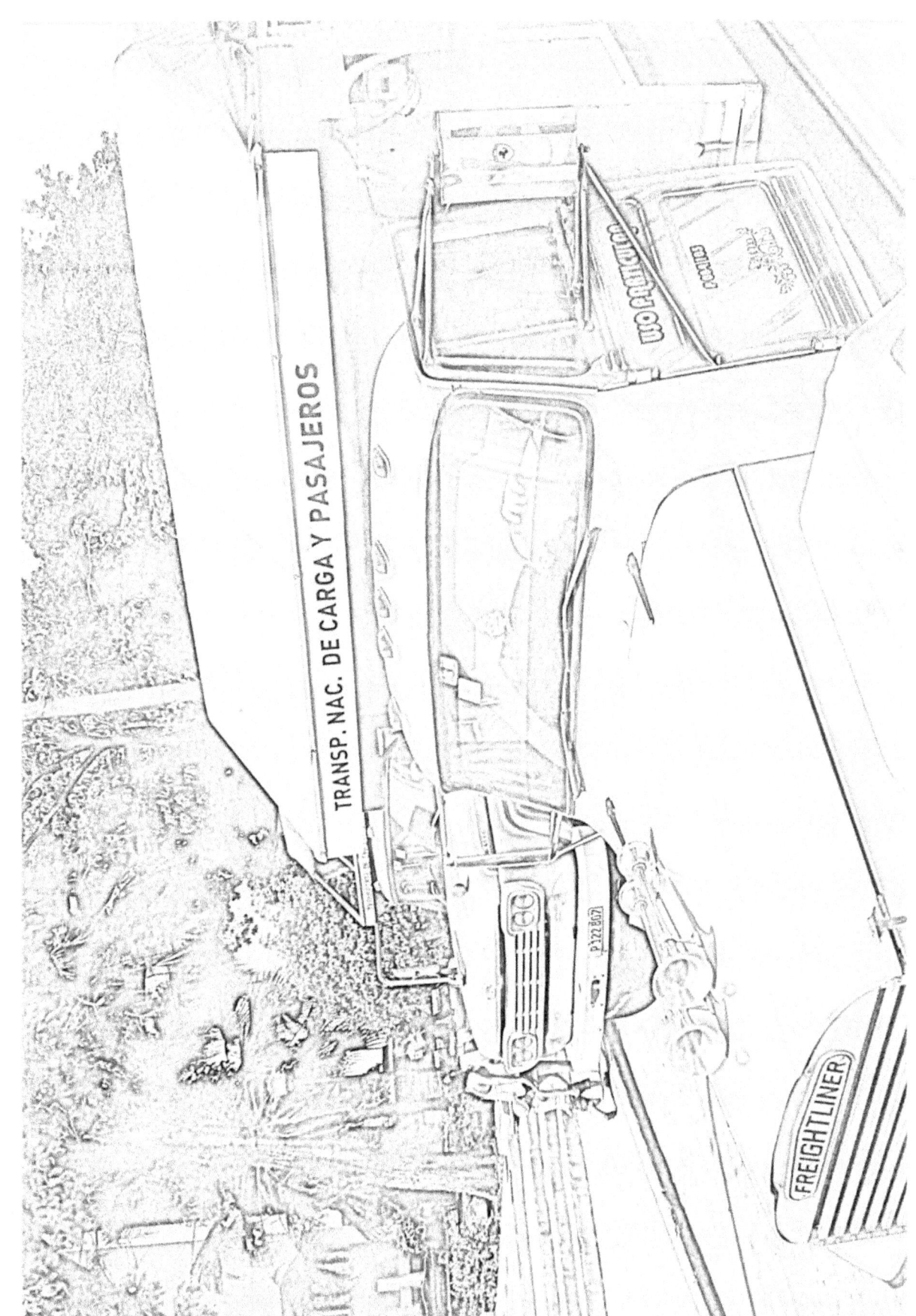

Private residence and tower near Marti Park in Cienfuegos, Cuba (now run by the state)

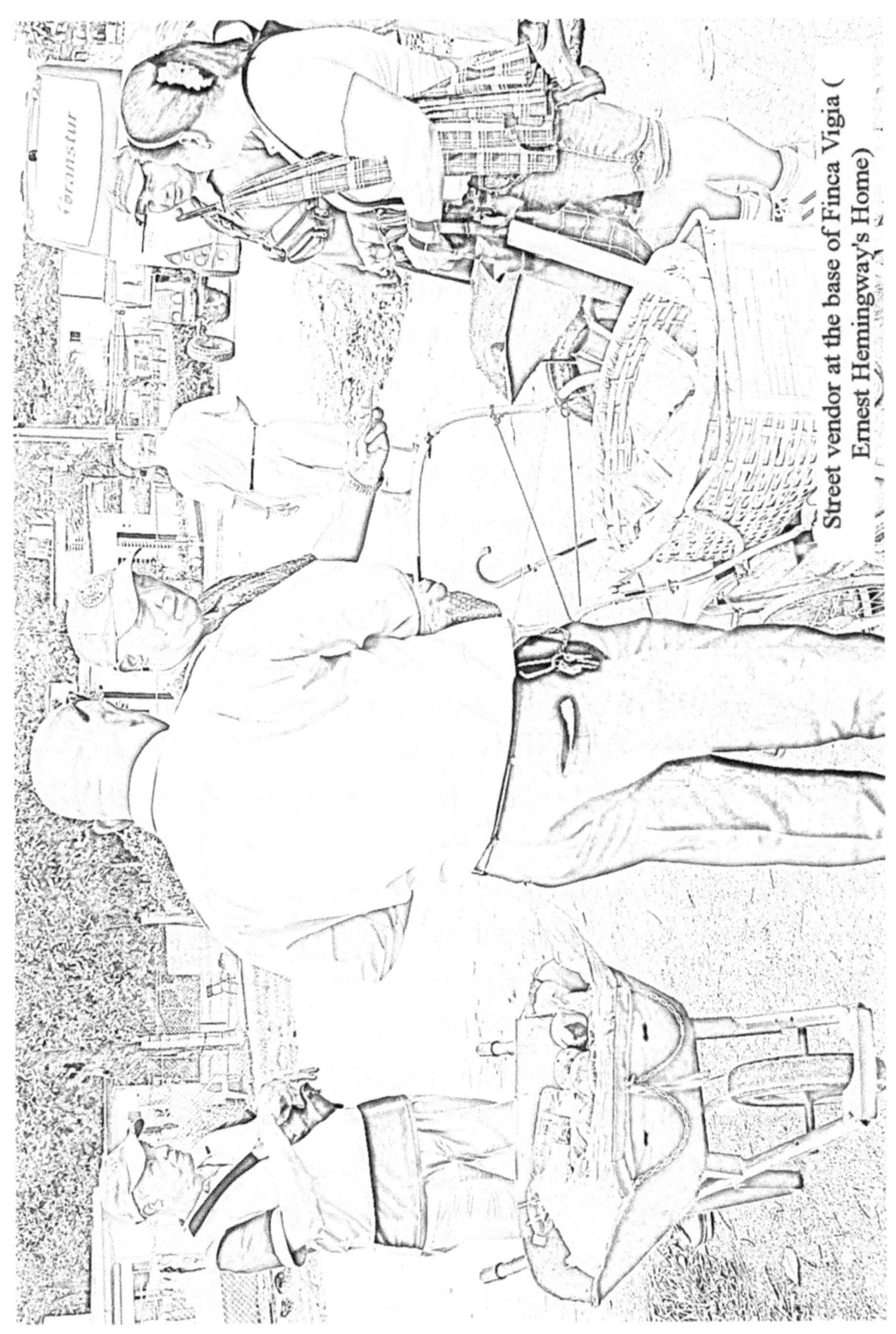

Street vendor at the base of Finca Vigia (Ernest Hemingway's Home)

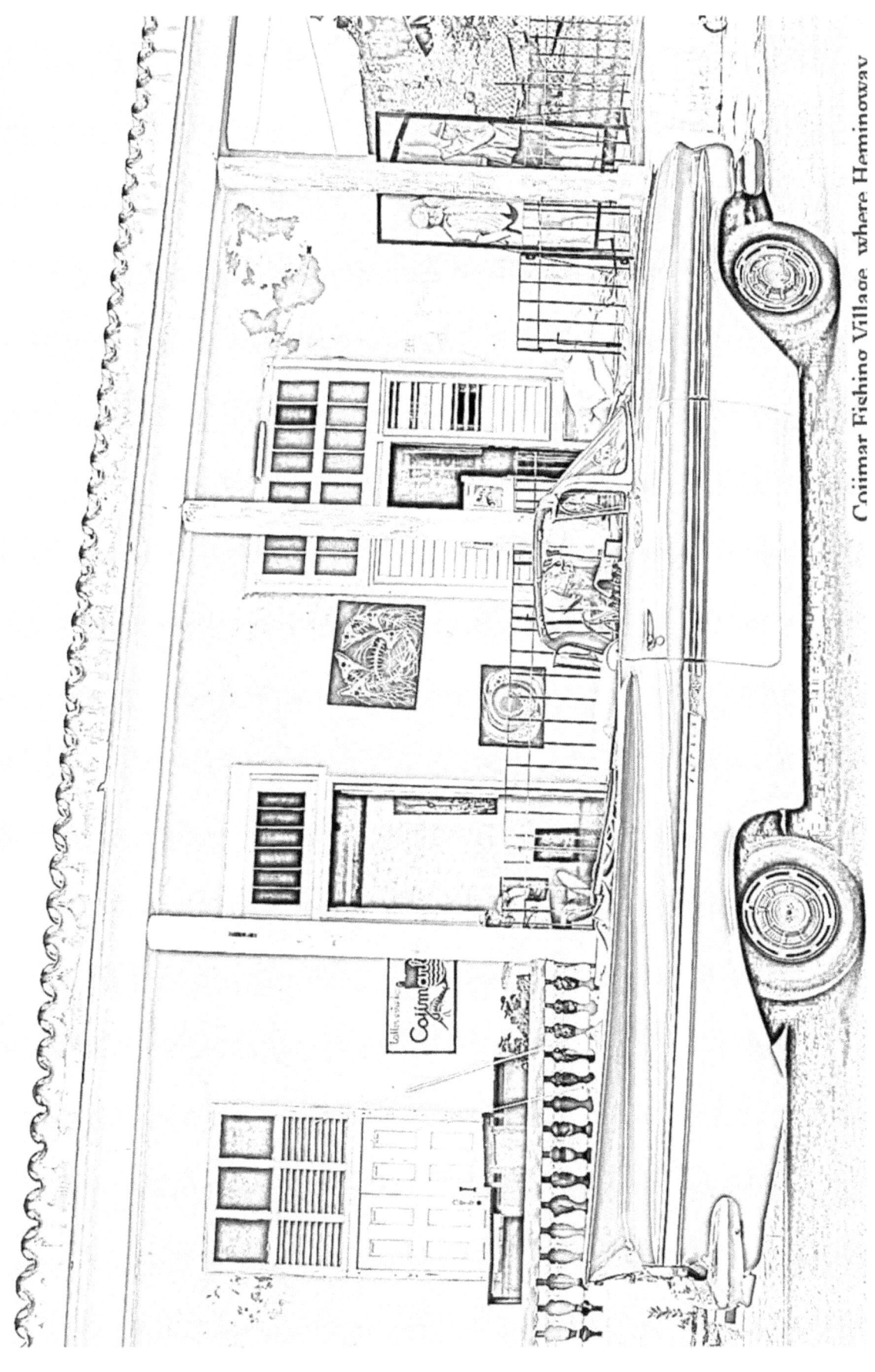

Cojimar Fishing Village where Hemingway

Vintage cars on avenue near Marti Park in Cienfuegos, Cuba

Street Cleaner on a road in Santiago de Cuba
(everyone is required to work in Cuba)

San Pedro de la Roca Lighthouse, Santiago de Cuba

Emilio Bacardi Family Museum (as in Bacardi Rum) Santiago de Cuba

Bruce Oliver near Vintage car at Finca Vigia (Hemingway's Home)

Vintage Car in artist José Fuster's neighborhood in Havana, Cuba

Cemetary Worker at the Necrópolis Cristóbal Colón - Havana, Cuba

Street vendors near Marti Plaza in Cienfuegos, Cuba

The Catedral de San Cristóbal, La Habana Plaza de la Catedral (Old Havana) Cuba

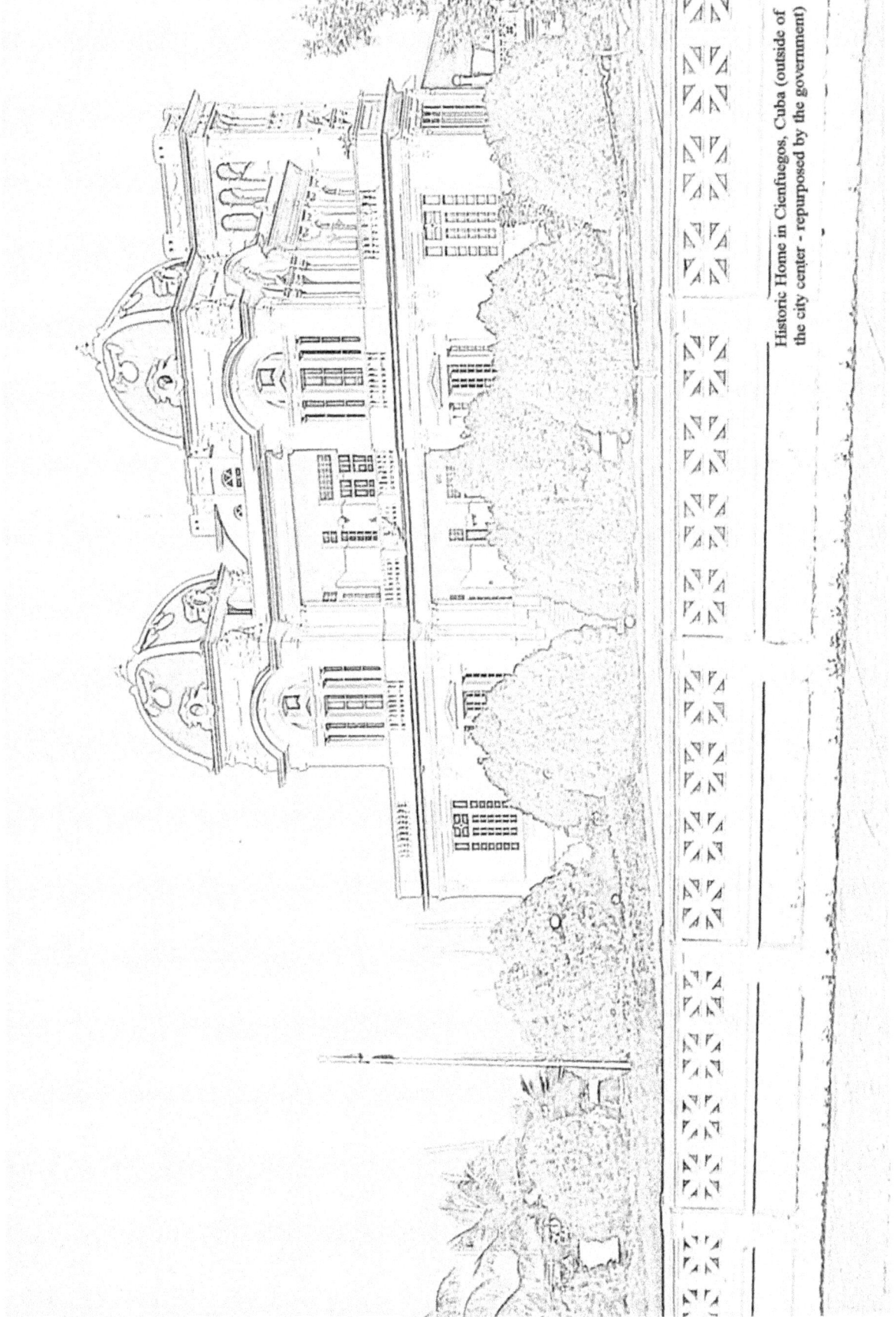

Historic Home in Cienfuegos, Cuba (outside of the city center - repurposed by the government)

Musicians outside of the Buena Vista Social Club - Santiago de Cuba

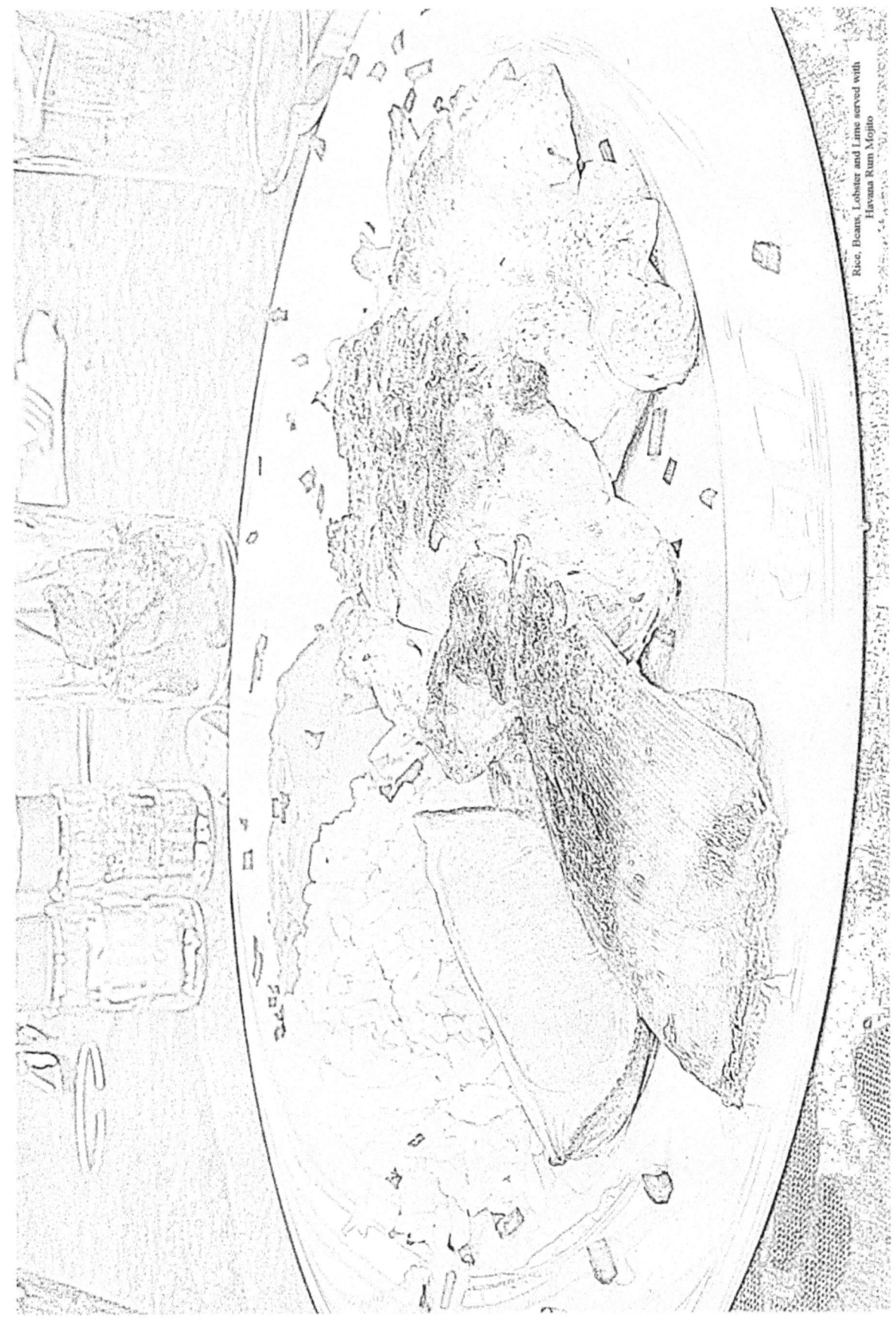

Rice, Beans, Lobster and Lime served with Havana Rum Mojito

Fountain and Bandshell in Marti Park - Cienfuegos, Cuba

Vintage cars along the Malecón / Sea wall in Havana, Cuba

www.ingramcontent.com/pod-product-compliance
Lightning Source LLC
LaVergne TN
LVHW061333060426
835512LV00017B/2673